# A New Beginning

A Survival Guide for Parents of

College Freshmen

Kaye Bernard McGarry, M.Ed.

A New Beginning: A Survival Guide for Parents of College Freshmen
Copyright © 2001 by Kaye Bernard McGarry, M.Ed.

Printed in the United States of America

All rights reserved. No part of this book may be reproduced or transmitted in any form or by any means, electronic or mechanical, including photocopy, recording, or any information storage or retrieval system, without the express written permission of the publisher. First printing 1997.

Second Edition 2001.

Published by: Survival in College Press
Charlotte, North Carolina

Library of Congress Catalog

Card Number: 2001-131030

ISBN 0-9661201-1-6

Book and Jacket Design: Spectrum Type & Art

Quantity discounts are available on bulk purchases of this book for educational training purposes, fund raising, or gift giving.

Address all inquiries to:
Survival in College Press
5101 Gorham Drive
Charlotte, North Carolina 28226-6405
Phone: 1-800-280-4880 x88
Email: kbmcg@carolina.rr.com

# Dedication

To my husband, Dennis, who taught me to strive for perfection, and my children Dennis Dean, Kathryn Denise, Deborah Dee, and Derek Duane who taught me how to grow as a person during their teenage years and how to grow as a family during the years after college. I also learned from them how to "lighten up," and determine what is really important in life.

To Dorothy Miles and Virginia McCullough, whose encouragement and advice gave me the motivation to complete this work.

To college freshmen, parents of college freshmen, professors and administrators on the various college campuses I visited, who shared their experiences from different perspectives.

# Contents

# Preface to the Second Edition

In this edition, I have expanded the chapters on communication, roommates, and managing finances, and added a chapter on "Connecting to the Workforce," but otherwise left the text much as it had been. Since publishing the first edition, I have conducted numerous seminars attended by hundreds of parents of high school students, parents of incoming college freshmen, and high school college bound seniors. I have also toured many college campuses, interviewed professors, administrators, parents, and students after they completed their freshman year.

I have also made a few changes and additions where I thought I could clarify a part of my subject matter better today than four years ago. I found the information in the first edition to be still appropriate today.

# Preface

The exciting but often frightening transition from the world of the high school senior to an identity as a college freshman is one of the most important adjustments many young adults must make. The results of this transition will affect virtually every aspect of a student's future.

Books dealing with parenting from birth through adolescence are plentiful; however, **A New Beginning: A Survival Guide for Parents of College Freshmen,** deals with the phase of life after adolescence, when one is considered, for all practical purposes, an adult, yet most are still financially dependent on parents for part, if not all, of their college expenses.

This book is for parents who will soon be or already are parents of college freshmen. It offers advice, help, and inspiration to parents, whether their students are enrolled at four-year colleges or universities, two-year colleges, or community colleges or technical schools.

Each phase of parenting is filled with many challenges and opportunities, and the same is true of the transition from high school to college. These challenges and opportunities are available for parents and their students. This book is an attempt to help parents understand what they and young adults face in this transition. It also shows parents how to offer helpful support to their college freshman.

First, parents must learn to let go. This is a process comparable to chapters in a book; students learn to close one chapter in order to begin the next. Parents need to do likewise in order to enjoy being a parent to an adult "child." When parents understand the transition, communicating with their children as adults will smooth the way to a new phase of the relationship.

It is my hope that after reading this book, parents will find a new beginning for their life after letting go, just as their students will find a new beginning as they start a new life as a college freshman. Your student needs the freedom, the responsibility, the independence that college life offers, yet he or she also needs the love and support of parents who can let go and understand what your college freshman is about to experience.

These can be wonderful times of growth for both you and your adult children. You are about to cross that bridge from parenting an adolescent to communicating with your young adult — your college freshman. Good luck, enjoy, and Godspeed!

*"Never, never, never give up."*
- WINSTON CHURCHILL

# Chapter 1

## FAITH IN YOURSELF AS PARENTS

After my first child left for college, I anxiously dialed his number to say hello. It had only been three days, but I was frantic. I had not heard from him yet. No letters. No phone calls. How was I to know he was okay? No answer. Where is he? I call at 8 a.m., noon, midnight, 2 a.m. Still no answer. By this time, I am extremely worried. Questions bolt through my head. He has a roommate, doesn't he? Someone must be in the room sometime. Does he sleep? Can he be partying so late at night? After what seems like days of getting no response by telephone to my son's room, in desperation I call the residence hall offices. An anonymous voice answers, but at least it is someone who can get a message to my son. My message is a simple one: Call home!

Hours later, the phone rang and I heard my son's happy and relaxed voice. "Hi, Mom. Are YOU okay?"

While it appeared he was safe, I, of course, had imagined the worst. Images of partying, drinking, being taken in by religious fanatics, an automobile accident, and even spending the night out with a girlfriend, raced through my mind.

When my first child left for college, I started a journey of parenting a college freshman that continued with each of my three younger children. Had I known then what my research has since taught me, I would have had the courage to let go from the start and would have realized that I had given my son, Dennie, ample tools to make decisions on the college campus. I would still communicate, but I would communicate with him as an adult on an adult level.

As is the case with many parents of the college freshman, I was too concerned about the ways I could continue to be part of his life. I also knew he needed the freedom to grow as an individual, and I was afraid I would try to interfere into his life too much. I needed some practical tips to help me deal with these changes.

As the months and years passed, I realized I was not alone. Most parents felt as I did. For parents in our position, a part of us was missing and we didn't want to let go. But after 18 years of parenting a child and adolescent, we didn't know how to make the transition.

Eventually, as each of my next three children departed for college, I not only learned to let go, I actually learned to enjoy the process.

Parents are not handed any "how to" books when they give birth to their children, leave the delivery room and head home with their babies. However, by the time the children are 18 or so, most parents have done quite a good job of parenting their child through childhood and adolescence. Despite their self doubts, parents usually do the best they can under the circumstances with which they are presented. Most children can deliver all our lectures! They can quote our "rules to live by," and they know our values. They have seen them at work over 18 years. Most children learn by what they see, as this poem, written by Dorothy Law Nolte, so aptly describes:

## Children Learn What They Live

*If a child lives with criticism, they learn to condemn. . .*
*If a child lives with hostility, they learn to fight. . .*
*If a child lives with pity, they learn how to feel sorry for themselves. . .*
*If a child lives with ridicule, they learn to be shy. . .*
*If a child lives with jealousy, they learn what envy is. . .*
*If a child lives with shame, they learn to feel guilty. . .*
*If a child lives with encouragement, they learn to be confident. . .*
*If a child lives with tolerance, they learn to be patient. . .*
*If a child lives with praise, they learn to be appreciative. . .*
*If a child lives with acceptance, they learn to love. . .*
*If a child lives with approval, they learn to like themselves. . .*

*If a child lives with recognition, they learn it is good to have goals. . .*
*If a child lives with sharing, they learn about generosity. . .*
*If a child lives with honesty and fairness, they learn what truth and justice are. . .*
*If a child lives with security, they learn to have faith in themselves and in those about them. . .*
*If a child lives with friendliness, they learn that the world is a nice place to live. . .*
*If a child lives with serenity, your child will live with peace of mind. . .*

When your child starts receiving college acceptance letters, the flurry of excitement — and confusion — reaches its peak. The college admissions process is well under way, and choosing a college becomes a challenge; when the choice is finally made, a quiet restlessness often sets in.

After high school graduation, the fears and worries begin for both parents and students. For parents, these questions sound something like this:

* *Will my daughter be successful?*
* *How can my son allot enough time to study?*
* *How prevalent are sex, alcohol, and drugs on the college campus?*
* *Will my daughter get lost in the shuffle and be only a social security number, rather than an individual?*
* *How will my son adapt when he is coming from a small high school and going to a large college or university?*

## Stages and Stresses

Barbara Neff, a campus minister from the University of North Carolina at Charlotte, says: "As parents, we need to let go, but I didn't want to. No parent wants to, but we must. When my first child left for college, I wrote her a letter every day for two months to compensate for what I felt was a lack of preparation in high school and also a lack of my preparation as a parent." She adds, "Among the students I deal with those with the most problems have parents who won't let go."

Barbara describes this as an "on your knees time in your life," and she prays a lot — many parents are like Barbara. Barbara also believed that her child, coming from a rural area, wasn't sophisticated enough to handle the barrage of choices on the college campus: whether to drink, how much to sleep, when to eat, and whether or not to go to classes. A freshman is coping with numerous choices and does not need additional pressure from parents.

Whether we believe it or not, our students have absorbed all our advice and good examples, so now is the time to let go and let them make the decisions. We have given them tools. How they use these tools in their college years and beyond is their responsibility. We will continue to encourage them, of course, but we let them decide each step along the way.

If you have faith that your children are capable of making good decisions, then they will probably make good decisions. As independent as these students think they are, the family ties are strong and they need to experience them as a part of their identity, but also be able to forge ahead to discover their own identity and way of life.

Many decisions young people make are neither right nor wrong, but somewhere in between. Your job is to learn to ask questions in a non-judgmental way. For example: Did you consider this? Have you thought of that? Open-ended questions usually work to open up communication: "What's happening in your life?" or, "How's it going at college?"

My daughter's first English paper was due the day she began printing it off the word processor. But then, her ribbon ran out of ink. She called home in distress – after all, it was the first week of school. In this case, she wanted Mom to make the decision for her and to solve her problem. As a parent of a college freshman in transition, I needed to ask some questions. Let's look at your options? What choices do you have? Which one seems the best one for you? Once she was calm and able to articulate some solutions to her dilemma, the problem no longer seemed so overwhelming. She found her best option. She was able to borrow a ribbon from another student in her residence hall who had the same kind of word processor. This example shows how we can facilitate the decision making process without making the decision for them.

Here's another example: Because of my son's Advanced Placement Math scores in high school, he was placed into an advanced math course at the university. When he called home to say he wanted to drop the course, some of the questions we asked him were: Why can't you master this course? Have you discussed this with your advisor and your course professor? What advice did they give you? What alternatives do you have for math? Are you within the time limits to drop or add courses without a penalty? If your final decision is to drop the course, will you be happy with that decision?

When students take complete ownership of their decisions, they are much better able to handle the consequences, good or bad. Over time and with practice, they should be able to make increasingly better decisions. The same is true for you. With practice, you should be able to talk with your student in a much less judgmental tone. But this takes time, so be patient with yourself.

In adapting to this new role, Dr. John E. Reinhold, D.S.W., of the University of North Carolina at Chapel Hill, suggests that parents look at the transition like a football game. Until now, parents are the coach and have been sending in the plays from the sidelines to their young adult, the quarterback. And the student ran them. Now it's time to start letting the student call his or her own plays. Parents can still call time-outs from the sidelines and even hold a conference and say, "Are you sure you know what you are doing?" Disagree if you need to, but discuss it and then let the student go back in and continue calling the plays for better or worse. Remember, college is only the pre-season. There is always room for improvement, and the real game will come after graduation.

When their children go off to college, parents change their role, which is a major shift during these years. Sometimes the quarterback doesn't want to follow his own game plan. He may say, "Wait a minute, send in a few more players. Call time out." Every year, though, the season is going to look better.

*"As long as you get an "A" for effort, that's the "A" that counts!"*

- BROOKE SHIELD'S DAD

# Chapter 2

# HOW TO COMMUNICATE WITH YOUR COLLEGE FRESHMAN

Relax, parents! You have done your job. Did you ever wonder why God gave us two ears and only one mouth? Listen more; talk less! Does this sound familiar? Now is the time to be that listening ear for your college students. They will go through some painful times, and change and transition can be difficult.

As parents, we need to communicate with our older children, not only before, but after they leave for college. Parents attending my seminars always ask, "How often should I call or visit?" They ask this question because they intuitively know that communication is important.

Kim, a freshman student at UNC-Chapel Hill, admitted to apprehensive feelings when she was preparing to start her freshman year.

"How am I going to know what to do when I get there and my Mom and Dad leave?", she asks herself. "Even though you always try to think of yourself as grownup and independent, when you get there, you feel how small you are. That was my greatest fear before I left for college."

Parents can alleviate some of these fears by establishing a pattern of communication, such as writing weekly letters by regular mail or e-mail. Students

7

welcome mail from home because it gives them a sense of continuity and helps them understand that they're still cherished by their family. One college administrator says parents would be surprised at how many college students sign up on junk mail lists just so they can have mail in their box. For some students, junk mail is better than no mail.

A word about e-mail. Computers have become an enormous part of college life and are used for everything from typing papers to registering for classes to doing research on the Internet. This means more students avail themselves of the opportunity to communicate with family and friends through e-mail. Many parents find that e-mail is the preferred way to communicate with their college student. One parent, a high school teacher, said that e-mail is the primary way she and her son keep up with each other. When my fourth child left for college, the university assigned him an e-mail address. There was no extra charge for this service and he could access his mail or use other features of this Internet connection from any computer learning lab on campus. I quickly invested in a modem for my computer at home and learned how to communicate by e-mail. Nowadays, many computers have a built-in modem. Service provider fees for usage are competitive, making e-mail quite economical. Some students in today's world just are not going to write a letter and send it through the mail, because e-mail is so easy.

For students with large families, scattered families, or divorced parents, e-mail is a way for the same letter to be copied and mailed to multiple addresses. This helps keep communication open and clear. Eventually, families will become familiar with a student's web site, be able to proofread papers if asked, or look over resumes. Some may even be able to send pictures if they know how to scan. New ways to use e-mail are being developed all the time, and communication is easier — and more economical — than ever before. So, consider all your options for communicating and choose a way that will best meet your needs and those of your student.

"Care packages" are another welcome sight, especially during exams or at other stressful times. Home-baked cookies or brownies mailed in an airtight container should stay fresh long enough to travel. Parents can choose a favorite holiday, such as Valentine's Day, and gather red and white balloons, jelly beans, candy hearts, streamers, napkins, and red Kool-aid packets, place them in a red box, tie a ribbon around it with a red heart with the words, "I love you" or "Just for you." At exam time, I have sent the following items for my youngest son in college. Bags of tortilla chips and salsa, peanut butter, home-baked cookies, chewing gum, candy, and dog biscuits for his beagle and black lab! Send fun care packages, not just those filled with practical items.

Phone calls are another way to continue the communication from home to college. However, be sensitive to the fact that many college students stay up late, so don't choose eight in the morning to call when you are fresh, wide awake and ready to go. Your student may not be so alert. You may reach your child, but, as one student pointed out, "Of course I'm in — I'm asleep!"

When you try to communicate by telephone, set up a time suitable for both of you. This helps eliminate such complaints as, "You're always checking up on me," or parents' concerns, "You're never in, so you must be partying all night." Students sometimes study in the library and most college libraries are open quite late. After normal closing hours, some libraries maintain a restricted area of the library with study tables, thereby giving students a place to study all hours of the night. College students and parents operate on different schedules — and we may as well adjust. One parent said she set aside Sunday afternoon for an hour phone call to each of her two daughters during all four years of college. Her daughters knew that time was reserved especially for them.

When your children do call home, listen — they will talk. During that first semester, everything is a crisis. But just as quickly as a crisis develops, it passes, especially once they have given you their problems to worry about. Crises sometimes occur after the first few weeks. This is the time students begin to get tired. Then they get sick, and then the midnight phone calls start. So, be prepared to listen, sympathize, and support, but then move on with your own life. In most cases, your young adults will already have moved on with their lives.

## To Visit or Not to Visit

Most colleges and universities host a parents' weekend in the fall which helps families give their students a sense of continuity. If your schedule allows, parents' weekend is a wonderful time to visit. Some students tell their parents how insignificant that weekend is and therefore, it is not important that they attend. However, listen to what they don't tell you. They may really want you there, but are sometimes timid about making a big deal of it. After all, they are told they are supposed to handle all the stress of college life on their own! Yet parents' weekend provides a meaningful opportunity for a family to communicate. In my experience, it's very worthwhile to go.

Parents' weekend can give you a glimpse of your children's life on campus. You see how they have decorated their room, meet their roommate and new friends, and see how they manage in their new environment. This is a good time to look into the window of college life your child is experiencing. You should come home with some idea of how well the transition from home to college has progressed.

Visiting at other times is usually welcome; however, unannounced visits are not appropriate. Just as you ask your friends and relatives before you visit, do extend the same courtesy to your young adult. As parents, you set the example and they will appreciate your thoughtfulness. One student wrote a short e-mail to his parents: "I'm learning a lot, studying hard, and acting responsibly. . . so no need for a surprise visit. . . especially this weekend. Okay?" We need to let go.

Parents also need to encourage their student to come home for fall break, since residence halls usually close on most campuses at this time. When students do come home, show interest in what they talk about. Generally, students have experienced the newness of college classes, the first cycle of studies, tests, and parties, so it is a good time to really listen, because they have encountered significant change. In some cases, six weeks at college may as well be six years.

Dr. Paul Burgett, Dean of Students at the University of Rochester in New York says: "Those first weeks of school are revolutionary in the life of the student. Everything has changed, but the symbols of that change are not obvious, because the child looks the same." The first visit home can be one of the most stressful visits for both parents and students. Therefore, you need to create meaningful opportunities for communication in order to avoid conflicts. Some potential areas of conflict are curfews, chores, and responsibilities. How you have progressed in learning how to communicate with your college student is critical at this point.

Some parents lament about the difficulty of communicating with young people who are not quite independent but are no longer adolescents. Single parents sometimes have a more difficult role to play in the transition. They often must be both father and mother, so communication becomes extremely important. All parents may have to spend more time than they are used to that freshman year listening to their young adult, but it will be worth the effort while your child is adjusting.

Parents who have only one child or whose youngest is leaving for college may also have additional difficulty with being willing to let go.

## Keeping the Channels Clear

Parents often ask: "How can I keep a channel of communication open? I feel as if I am letting go, but my college student is still turning me off." Does this sound familiar?

This dilemma usually is rooted in the way you communicate. Let's look at seven basic communication styles. They aren't new — we've been using them for 18 years! However, they won't work with college freshmen — they simply are no longer valid.

**1. You're General Patton.** "You're going to do what I tell you and you're going to do it RIGHT NOW!" General Patton's toughness and rough speech earned him the nickname "Old Blood and Guts." How many of us fall into this pattern of communicating with our kids? After so many years, it may be a difficult habit to break, but it is time to make the transition to better communication.

**2. You're Goldie Hawn.** We all like to be around people who make us happy. Goldie Hawn once said that when she was born "God went bing! Okay, you're going to be happy. You've got that little button of joy, and now you're going to pass it around." The parents who fall into this category respond with "m'm, m'm," do a million other things except listen when their teenager is trying to talk to them. These parents think they are paying attention, but they are oblivious to the real needs of their teenager. Perhaps they are cooking dinner, putting clothes in the dryer, answering the phone, scolding a younger child, scooting the dog out of the kitchen, reading the newspaper, listening to the evening news on television, and on and on. Meanwhile, the teen doesn't think anyone is listening.

**3. You're Perry Mason.** These parents are the investigators. Where are you going? When will you be home? Who are you going with? How much drinking has been going on? Why are you home late? When are you going to clean up your room? Why are you being rude and disrespectful to your parents? After three questions, the teens stop responding and the communication line is closed.

**4. You're Pollyanna.** Hayley Mills played this part in the movie. With her perfectly braided hair, she was full of wide-eyed curiosity and boundless, bubbly enthusiasm, always just "uncorked." The parents in this category constantly say, "Today is going to be a wonderful day. Everything will come out perfect!" But, realistically, parents know that sometimes everything is not wonderful and each day doesn't end up perfect. Our kids need that listening ear.

**5. You're Bill Cosby.** Cosby is the famous comedian and actor, who, as his characters, tells jokes all the time. Parents in this category are always responding to their teen with a funny joke. However, there are times when teenagers really want to talk seriously; perhaps your children have something they want to share with you and attempts at humor shut down the channel of communication. A joking response may no longer be appropriate, especially when a problem is potentially serious.

**6. You're Sigmund Freud.** The father of psychoanalysis, Freud revolutionized our ideas about how the human mind works. The parent who communicates in this manner is generally very theoretical and analyzes everything. They might say, "Now let's sit down here together to actually discuss your behavior this evening and try to discover some options for you to choose from in order to acquire more acceptable behavior patterns." Parents in this category have read all the self-help books: *All Grown Up and No Place to Go, I'm O.K., You're O.K., All I Really Need to Know I Learned in Kindergarten, Raising Children for Success*, and *The Secret of a Good Life with Your Teenager*. Try to go beyond analyzing everything and just accept your teenagers for who they are — and listen.

**7. You're Oral Roberts.** He is the American missionary and revivalist whose preaching made him known in many parts of the world. If you're not sure whether you fall into the preaching category, let me help you. If you try to get a point across to your teenager in three minutes and fifteen minutes later, you are still trying to get the same point across, you have become Oral Roberts.

These communication styles *turn off* the conversation. As parents of college students, we need to make a transition, and communicate on an adult-to-adult level. This is how we come to enjoy our college students now and long after they've graduated. Consider changing from parents "governing your kids" to parents "talking with your young adults."

*"I know you believe you understand what you think I said, but I'm not sure you realize that what you heard is not what I meant."*

\- ANONYMOUS

## Some Helpful Hints

If you fall into any of the communication styles listed above, now is the time to change the way you communicate. Doing so will help you enjoy your adult children now and long after they have graduated from college. As you think about changing habits, consider ways to keep the conversation going, or techniques to open up conversations. Some openers might include:

* *This sounds important to you.*
* *Tell me more about it.*
* *Would you like to talk about it now?*
* *I'd be interested in your point of view.*

Some responses to help keep a conversation moving along include:

* *I see . . .*

* *Really . . .*

* *You did? You do?*

* *Interesting . . .*

Some phrases to use when asking questions might include:

* *What do you think about . . .*

* *In your opinion . . .*

* *How do you feel about . . .*

If you try these suggestions — or others — remind yourself to think about how you are communicating before you start your next conversation with your student.

In addition, ask yourself, "Am I actively listening?" In active listening you

* *keep your talk to a minimum; in other words, don't talk too much.*

* *give your full attention; make eye contact; practice really listening.*

* *acknowledge what you are hearing; make some type of response.*

Research shows that one of the most common complaints from teens is that their parents don't listen. The best way to become a good active listener is to practice, practice, practice. Listen more carefully. Maybe there is a reason we have two ears and only one mouth. Try shifting your communication style from that of an "adult-to-child" type of communication to an "adult-to-adult" type of communication. When you make that shift, the relationship building of your children really begins and will then last a lifetime. Trust me, the effort is worth it. In the final analysis, your children will eventually become your best friends.

*"Education is what survives when what has been learnt has been forgotten."*

- B. F. SKINNER

# Chapter 3

## THE COLLEGE CAMPUS - THEN AND NOW

Each year, approximately 1.9 million American students head off to the college campus as freshmen.

The college campus that some parents attended might have been characterized by: dorms locked at midnight; strict curfews; single sex dorms, with no visitors of the opposite sex allowed; P.D.A. (public displays of affection) limited to hugging and kissing and sleeping around was considered unacceptable; and alcohol was prevalent to some extent but drug use was virtually invisible, and certainly not an acceptable pattern of behavior. Class attendance was taken and generally three cuts from a class carried a penalty of a one-letter drop of the final grade in that class. Supervision was plentiful from professors, resident assistants, resident directors, deans, and others on the college campus. These days are gone — and have been for 25 years or more — except in some small private schools.

Today, college students work with a 24-hour schedule. Many live in co-ed residence halls. Some even share co-ed bathrooms. Students have no penalties for class cuts; in fact, in most classes, attendance is not even taken. After all, it is the student's responsibility to attend class; it is the professor's responsibility to teach.

Alcohol and drug abuse is rampant on many of today's campuses. Date rape and other crimes are virtually out of control. There is no supervision and certainly no curfews. Many parents — the baby boomers — grew up in this college environment. That's one reason why they fear for their own children.

Student pressures may be the same, but the conditions under which those pressures are experienced and decisions are made are, in many cases, vastly different. Therefore, students must be "street smart" and have strong values. They must be clear about their direction in order to achieve their goals, without being hindered by too many of the distractions of college life.

Recent studies have discovered that many students are less prepared to cope with life and the stresses of college than students who attended college 20 years ago. Today, many are better prepared academically; however, they seem to possess fewer coping mechanisms. One reason can be that too much has been taken on or been done for them. As children, parents have solved many problems for them. So, as a young adult, when a crisis or difficulty arises, they are less prepared to deal with it successfully. Many students certainly are more worldly and are more sophisticated than in years past. However, their inability to cope has become more and more evident in this fast-paced and technologically advanced world we live in.

Many college campuses are microcosms of society and therefore experience problems similar to many communities. Concerns about the personal safety of your young adult are certainly valid.

There are variations in what constitutes safety on contemporary college campuses. Most campuses today have their own police force, which patrols and monitors the campus 24 hours a day. In addition, some have officers who patrol certain parts of campus on foot at night. During student orientation on most campuses, sessions on personal safety are required for all incoming students.

Escort services are also common on many campuses. Students can call any time during night-time hours and are escorted from one location to another, and call boxes are located throughout most campuses. The awareness of crime and the need to use common sense when students are out and about is very important. Freshmen will adapt to the conditions on their particular campus, but for the first few weeks they need to be conscious of safety procedures as they become acclimated and "street wise."

When you visit the campus, read the college newspapers, talk with your child's new friends, read the bulletin boards in campus centers and look at the graffiti on the bathroom walls. The college campus of today is still an exciting place to be; however, it may be different from what parents remember.

*"Everyone receives 24 hours a day, 168 hours a week regardless of origin, position in life, or particular circumstances. If we are honest with ourselves, most of us can learn just about anything 'IF' we give ourselves enough time."*

-AUTHOR UNKNOWN.

# Chapter 4

# TIME AND STUDY MANAGEMENT: A NEW CHALLENGE FOR COLLEGE FRESHMEN

When parents of college freshmen talk to parents whose children are sophomores, juniors, or seniors, they are often amazed at the poor GPA's (grade point average) some seemingly bright, intelligent kids are coming home with. These are kids who were among the top achievers in high school. They ask me to help them understand why this is happening.

Managing time in college is one of the biggest challenges for all college freshmen. Studies show that poor use of time is the biggest single reason that freshmen do not maintain at least a C average. Surveys of undergraduate students continually show that 70 percent or more of the students report that their greatest personal need is to manage time more effectively.

A senior with an elementary education major says, "Survival in college is a management skill that people are never taught." She learned one survival tool on her own, however. She observed students who were tested for dyslexia being taught how to take notes. From these observations, she developed her own system of taking notes.

The following is a list of high school seniors' concerns about leaving for college.

This list is compiled and updated each year when I speak to various groups of high school seniors during the spring of their senior year. Generally, by this time, the college admissions process is complete and most of them know where they will be headed in the fall. "Senioritis" has set in and students are no longer listening to parents, teachers, or counselors. But, they are open to listening to an outside resource like me. I speak to them about the transition from being a high school senior to being a college freshman, and generally ask them to get into groups of three or four. Then I say: "Let's pretend that it is August 15th; you are packed for college. You're all ready to go, but you're still scared to death, worried, or anxious about *something* — but what?" Then each group jots down three or four things that come to mind. Below are the most common things, listed in the order of frequency mentioned.

Roommate

Food

Getting lost

Money/finances

Meeting people, making friends, social life

Managing time

Date rape

Leaving home-family and friends

Laundry

Choosing classes

Difficulty of course work

What to wear and what to pack

Part-time jobs

Studying/how much?

Teachers/professors

Failing

Grades

Picking a major

Clubs/organizations/athletics

Basically, the three top concerns or anxieties are emotional in nature.

They are: 1. Roommate; 2. Food; and 3. Getting Lost. Even though we know these concerns are emotional, as we leave our kids on the college campus we parents still say:

Study hard.

We're paying big bucks.

Give it 100 percent.

Do your best.

These are common statements from parents. Most of the time, both parents and students want the same thing — academic success. But, as you can see from the above list, studies are near the bottom of the list of concerns right now. Students have a transition period to work through first. They have to meet some of the needs that are most important to them, such as making new friends, before they can settle down to the business of academic success.

Crisis can be defined as a dramatic emotional upheaval in a person's life. As you can see, most of the concerns listed are emotional in nature, and the transition is an emotional upheaval. However, if before coming to the campus your student is aware of the opportunities and challenges the college transition can bring, that student will have a much better chance of confidently and successfully working through the transition.

When I ask parents to list their major concerns about their students leaving for the college campus, the top three concerns are: (1) Self-discipline to schedule enough time to master their studies; (2) Partying too much; and (3) Safety and security on campus and off. So, academics are on top of the parent lists, yet on the bottom of the student lists.

One parent, whose child failed Freshman English, asked, "Did you study?" In tears, the student said, "No, but I never had to study in high school. I only had to go to class to make straight As."

This is a familiar scene, since students often think college will be just like high school. If both parents and students want academic success, then students need to come up with a time-management plan to achieve academic success. They need to create a schedule and learn how to follow it, especially during their freshman year.

As parents, we need to understand many of the reasons why freshman students have so much trouble managing their time. A schedule that helps students organize their time is important because in high school things were different. Students were in class approximately 30 hours a week and many students completed their homework during class time. In college, students are in classes approximately 15 hours a week. In high school, students have approximately 10-15 grades during a nine-week grading period and in many cases, the teacher drops the lowest grade. In college, many will have 14-week semesters with two tests or three tests and a final. Since essay tests take so long to grade, many tests will be multiple choice. Students enrolled in many of the required courses on college campuses may have as few as 20 or as many as 350 students in one class. For some, their entire high school had 350 students. Taking notes and concentrating in these large classes is different from their high school experience. One student, a freshman at Samford University, found it helpful to sit in front of the class. "Sounds nerdy, I know," he said, but he learned that's what it took to make him focus. All students must find their own ways to help them stay focused.

After failing his first test in Honors Political Science, a student at the University of Georgia called home collect and said, "Come get me because I'm not college material." His parents said, "Buck up. We're not coming to get you. Go see your professor." When he did, his professor helped him learn how to read the material, how to best listen to his lectures, and offered tips on how to take the next test. The student did everything the professor suggested and made the highest grade in the class. He learned a powerful lesson — how to learn.

As parents, we know that high school seniors have learned to work the system in high school. They study the night before a test, and most of what they study is memorization. Now, just put yourself inside the head of young people in September. They are off to college; they have new clothes; they have a little money in their pocket, since it is the first week on campus. They need friends, right? You have seen the syllabus for each course and you can see that for some classes mid-October may be the first test and it's a mid-term exam. No other quizzes, graded material, or reports may be due. So realistically, the freshmen may not have tests in any classes until mid-October. And, they need friends, right? You can begin to see how the crisis develops.

Many of us had enforced discipline during our college days. Remember having three cuts in a class and then our grade was lowered? The dorms may have been locked at midnight, and there were probably no co-ed dorms. Today, no one is there to impose discipline. There is no curfew; on many campuses the residence halls never close; many residence halls are co-ed. Discipline is all up to the student. It's self-discipline. That's the source of the tremendous pressure your student experiences.

# Time Management—The Key to Success

A counselor at Appalachian State University says the biggest concern she sees for college freshmen is time management. At college, they have 24 hours to manage; at home, most students didn't have to do that, because there was at least a loose schedule for meals, laundry, school, and work. All of a sudden students find that college life presents a 24 hour day in which they can do anything they please. This becomes overwhelming for many freshmen, because they are not prepared for time management. Many parents tell me that their biggest concern about their student is his or her ability to manage their time.

All experts tell us that if students study one hour per class hour, they can expect to get a C average. If they study 2-3 hours per class hour, they can expect to get an A or a B. So, the pressure is on. They need friends, they need to study, and they may not have exams or papers due before mid-October. Generally, I tell high school seniors that the rising sophomore students advise new freshmen to do three things during their freshmen year in order to be successful:

**1. Make a schedule (See Appendix I for sample schedule).** List the class hours using an X for class hours. Then list the study hours using an S for study hours and base the number of study hours on the criteria mentioned above. Most freshmen will have 15 hours of class time; therefore, they need to schedule at least 30 hours of study time, depending on their goals. They may not always hold to their schedule — they may mess up one week. That might be okay. However, if they mess up their schedule for a second week, they could be in trouble and they may not be able to get themselves back on schedule. If they decide to go out with friends during a time clearly marked S for study, they need to move that S time into another time slot — this is of critical importance.

**2. Read.** It is common to have to read 30 to 40 pages per night per class. Reading is difficult for some students, because reading takes patience. Many kids today lack the patience to read for long periods. Television has contributed to this, because today's young people are used to seeing everything happen on television in 30 to 60 minute time slots. Life situations are presented and solved during these brief periods — they have seen entire wars fought and won in a three-night mini-series! Thus, students need to learn to use some of their study time for focused reading.

**3. Study class notes.** In order to study their notes, they need to take notes. In order to take notes, they must be in class, especially during that first semester.

Notes are like gold. Many of the tests and exams given in college have all their questions taken from the class lectures. So, students need to use some of their study time to really absorb their class notes. A good note-taker is always analyzing, actively seeking to find out what the professor is really talking about. Key ideas are written down in a short, concise manner, but without writing every word the professor says.

These are the challenges freshmen face in managing their time successfully. To a great extent, the schedule they create will determine how successful they intend to be that first semester and beyond. How well they *follow* their schedule will determine their actual success.

*"It's not so important what I am; it's what I'm becoming that's important."*

# Chapter 5

## THE FIRST VISIT HOME

Consider making some adjustments in your household rules, when your college freshman returns home for the first time. Some students complain to college administrators that they don't feel quite right about being treated the way they were when they were seniors in high school and living at home.

Changes for freshman are so great in such a short period of time, but parents' lives remain relatively unchanged. Even such a simple thing as students coming home and doing the laundry a bit differently can bring criticism from parents. As parents, we need to make some adjustments for this first visit and beyond.

I suggest deciding what adjustments will fit into your household before your student comes home for that first visit. Then share your thoughts with your student to make that adjustment smooth for everyone.

Cindy, a freshman at Wofford, says, "I never did laundry at home. Now, coming home after my first year at college, my Mom won't do it, so, I have to. It's a real pain." However, Cindy realized that some changes were needed and responsibilities reassigned. On the other hand, Sonnet, a freshman at Ohio University, says she had to do her own wash as a senior in high school. That way she was better prepared for this responsibility. In a single-parent household, many students have been handling this chore for many years. Single parents sometimes need to share chores and responsibilities, and students in these families often learn to become self-sufficient a lot sooner than many young people.

Is a parent-imposed curfew still relevant to your now adult child when that adult has been living on a college campus and is learning how to manage time? I recommend treating them as adults and easing these rules.

At the same time they need to respect your general house rules, those rules that make your home run smoothly. Work out a way where they feel they have control over their own lives, but you are still able to maintain a household based on respect for each other's needs. For example, if your student plans to come in at 2 a.m., perhaps an agreement can be worked out for a quiet entrance where no one is disturbed, especially family members who may need to rise early for work. Just as we let people in our household know where we are and when we will return, suggest that as a courtesy for your adult student. Build mutual respect on an adult-to-adult level.

Students' schedules on a college campus are vastly different from your schedule at home. They need the leeway to decide how to manage their hours at home. They also need to know you have faith in their decisions about when to go out and when to come home. They are growing and changing at a rapid rate during this transition process. However, they also need to respect your wishes, whatever you decide, because it is still your own household. Consider making some adjustments, though.

Kristin, a freshman at Appalachian State University, says, "My parents realized I didn't have restrictions on me when I was at college, so when I went home they didn't question me about where I was going when I went out. However, my Mom would tell me I wasn't going out until I cleaned up my room or did laundry, or some other chore I used to do in high school while living at home. When it came to household chores, they didn't treat me any differently than when I was in high school."

As parents, recognize that your children have changed. You will still recognize them, but, they will be different. Your student has been away from home and has had a vastly different experience being on a college campus. Parents just haven't had a chance to catch up with the changes in their students' lives. Make changes that will fit into your household; take time to talk with the young adults, but don't let them run over you.

One parent of a student at the University of Georgia says that when her daughter came home for the first time she was more communicative than she had been in two years. "It was as if she was 'chatty kathy,' and was so excited about everything. She was willing to talk — she wanted to talk — and even shared things we didn't want to know. She wanted us to know what she was going through in her freshman year."

Robert, a freshman at Samford University, tells about his experience during the Christmas break. "I would have all these things that happened at college that I was so excited about and my parents asked some questions, but not about my interests. They mostly asked about academics. It wasn't until just before I went back to campus that my Dad and I finally talked about college in a real sense, and that was nice." Robert wanted to share his experiences with his parents. He also needed assurance that his parents still loved him and cared about him.

In a recent survey of college freshmen, I asked the following questions:

(1) What was the most effective thing families did to provide encouragement and support?

(2) How can freshmen balance the freedom of college with the structure of home when they return there during the first year?

*Refer to Appendix IV for a list of some of their responses.*

*"Education and persistence are the keys to success, no matter what your goal."*
- BILL COSBY

# Chapter 6

## HELPING STUDENTS LEARN HOW TO HANDLE THEIR FINANCES

You have just paid the college tuition and room and board and now your student is asking for more money. Sound familiar? Students in college have the added stress of managing their money, many times without financial help from their parents.

The decision about who pays for what needs to be clear, and this decision will vary greatly from family to family. It is important that you tell your children what portion of their college expenses *they* will be responsible for. They need to know what their limits are and what they must contribute. Students sometimes work in the summer to earn money for their college expenses, and parents may believe their student needs to hold a job during the school year, too.

Before our oldest child, Dennie, left for college, we expected him to save $1,500 to use as spending money during his freshman year. When he came home for Christmas, he had already depleted his funds, but he was able to work over the holidays to replenish his bank account. Gradually, he learned how quickly money can disappear. He was also learning the importance of a budget. Whatever the financial arrangements in your household, parents and students need to discuss and understand the budgeting process. After all, a college education is very expensive.

Sit down and prepare a sample budget with your student. *(Refer to Appendix II for Sample Budget)*. Inevitably, there will be some unexpected expenses that you can't anticipate, but a sample budget will provide a basic tool to get started. Then, when a question arises about who can pay for an unanticipated expense, you can both go back to your sample budget as a tool to start your discussion about why you can or cannot provide additional funds. It also helps the student understand how financial planning works.

Sometimes, you may want to provide some discretionary funding for something you think may be worthwhile, even though your budget indicates that this was supposed to be your student's expense. For example, as a freshman, Dennie asked for financial help for a weekend ski trip sponsored by the Newman Catholic Center at UNC. He had volunteered to help on a fundraising committee at the Newman Center during his first semester. He was using the "how to manipulate Mom and Dad" skills we all learned growing up! It would have been easy to say no. After all, it was clear he was to earn all his spending money, because we were providing his tuition and room and board. However, as a parent of a new college freshman, my heart said yes. We would help in a small way. I consider this "discretionary" funding. Some parents might have said no and that would be fine, too. Some parents have no room for discretionary funding or for extras in a family budget that is already overburdened. As parents, you have choices about spending your money. But, that is also why the best path is to make expense sharing clear right from the start.

If Dennie had asked for money for a ski trip he was organizing on his own, my answer clearly would have been no and would have remained no. However, in the case mentioned above, I believed he was attempting to get involved in a student organization on his college campus and there were adults accompanying the group, in case of emergencies. Therefore, I could justify his involvement in this particular organization, because it would pay dividends later. And so it did. Through this organization, he met many college friends of his own faith who served as a positive support group. He grew as a person by taking a leadership role. He identified a niche whereby he could connect to the university, on a campus so large that one could easily get lost in the crowd.

Encourage your student to discover a niche on campus by joining a club or organization that matches his or her interests. One student was interested in politics and student government, so she ran for hall representative in her residence hall. It was a niche that enabled her to explore a special interest. Another student volunteered as a photographer for the student newspaper. This meant that he had passes to many of the sports games, plays, and other activities he was interested in because he was covering them for the newspaper. He was finding a suitable niche on his campus and was meeting people at the same time.

## Telephone Expenses

Parents always ask, "What is the best, most cost effective way to handle heavy phone use?" Parents and students need to refer to the sample budget in the appendix to determine who is responsible for the phone expense. Are you willing to pay the monthly telephone service fee for local phone calls? Are you willing to pay an agreed upon amount per month for long distance calls? Determine the answer to those questions, and depending on who is funding what portion of the bill, heavy phone use will generally fall into perspective early during the freshman year. Adjustments may take time, but generally, these issues work themselves out.

In our case, we agree to pay for local calls, which includes the monthly service fee to have a telephone. On some campuses, there is no additional charge for a room phone. We also have a 800 number at no additional charge, so our students are able to call home. It cannot be used for any other numbers. However, they cover other long distance calls. It is up to them how much or how little to use the phone for long distance calls, and this is another learning experience. Remember, too, that e-mail is another economical alternative.

## Banking Skills

Many freshmen open a checking account for the first time. Parents know the bank explains in the fine print how to manage a new bank account, but many students receive the first bank statement and simply file it, assuming that nothing more needs to be done.

The bank statements pile up until Thanksgiving or Christmas break. At that time, parents may sense some confusion when they ask about the current status of the student's financial affairs. Parents hear the students disclose with amazement that the bank balance for their checking account doesn't agree with what they really have in the bank! Many seem perplexed, as if the bank must be wrong. Of course, some have not even bothered to record all checks and most never keep a running balance in their check register. Some don't even know what a check register is. One college freshman had these entries:

**Kangaroo Candy $2.26**

**Rocky's $6.10**

**Classic City Cleaners $6.00**

**Steveninos Restaurant $5.70**

**Peking Restaurant $6.00**

**Belk's Department Store $7.88**

**Vision Video $3.40**

**Kroger Grocery $8.48**

**Golden Pantry $1.78**

**Payless Gas $11.54**

**Cookie Company $.83**

Don't be surprised. This is quite typical of many freshmen. A customer service representative from one of the banks says that many students don't realize they are charged a service fee every time they use another bank's ATM machine. Yet, if they had walked one more block, they may have found a bank machine from their own bank, where there would be no additional service charge to conduct any transaction. Convenience is very important to these students. When their bank statement comes in, when and if they look at it, the typical response is, "Why do I have this charge?"

One of the most difficult adjustments for a student at East Carolina University was managing money. Her monthly spending allowance from monies she earned herself was 140 dollars, which she spent the first two weeks at college. Her long distance calls to her boyfriend at North Carolina State University totaled 150 dollars. By the end of the first semester, her Dad said, "Whoa, we need to talk!"

One student withdrew 10 dollars from her account through the teller machine. Her balance appeared, indicating she had "200 extra dollars." She said "WOW" and proceeded to spend some of that. The fact that some of her checks may not have gone through the bank process never occurred to her. In reality, she did not have that 200 extra dollars.

A parent of three says her oldest is finally graduating from Wake Forest University after five years and several changes in major. She is graduating on the dean's list, yet she can't even balance a checkbook! Her daughter, along with many other students, is just taking a longer time to mature.

Another parent gave his son a checking account for high school graduation. He found it helpful to have the summer to learn to manage his account with his parents available to answer questions about bank statements and charges.

Students sometimes say, "If my Mom or Dad had only explained the banking process to me. . ." and parents often ask me about the best way to help their young adults set up a personal finance program. Parents can help by showing their students how to balance a checkbook and read a bank statement, or by having them make an appointment with the customer service representative at their bank. All banks are happy to sit down with the student and explain the instructions for reconciling a bank statement, and students may actually listen to a person who isn't their parent.

Students struggle for independence during the college years, but many times they are financially dependent upon their parents for their college expenses. Besides tuition and room and board, student expenses range from books, meals, and fraternity and sorority dues to dry cleaning, laundry, gasoline, and telephone. Refer again to the sample budget, which can help both students and parents discuss money management.

As much as I tried to look at college expenses for my sons and daughters in equal terms, I found there definitely were additional expenses incurred by my daughters. Clothing needs, cosmetics, and toiletries just seem to be higher with daughters. However, we still tried to use the same budgeting techniques. Basically, we covered their actual *needs*; they had to earn money for their *wants*.

There are some students, however, who by necessity must earn 100 percent of their college expenses. For these students it is even more important to discuss money matters and help them learn how to devise a budget, adjust it when needed, yet still come out with a balanced budget at the end of their freshmen year.

Parents can help to avoid conflicts in the area of money management and budgeting by being honest about family finances and clear about their expectations before their child leaves for college.

A budget, excluding tuition and room and board, is included in Appendix II. You can already see how even a budget that looks this simple can provide food for thought and open a discussion about spending habits. After all, students are coming from vastly different lifestyles, and they need to understand how to manage their money. The sample budget should help put into perspective some of the choices students have in learning how to manage their own money.

Decide who is paying for what and be aware of the hidden expenses. For example, when living at home, soap, toothpaste, shampoo, pencils, pens, transportation costs, paper, kleenex, paper towels, and toilet paper are generally absorbed into the family budget. Are you willing to continue to furnish these items and replenish them each time they come home? Or, are these items you can give them as gifts on special occasions? Refer to Appendix III for gift ideas. Will they bring clothes home, believing the dry cleaning expense will come out of the family budget, or is this their expense as a college freshman? The phone bill is a biggie. Not many kids are used to paying their own phone bills and they may be making long distance calls to friends they weren't making before, because their friends were in their hometown.

## Credit Card Spending

Currently, credit cards are mailed directly to college students and often do not even require a completed application. Students are lured into taking credit cards with the offer of "free" gifts, just for accepting a credit card.

In *Futures* magazine, I read about a young man named Michael, who provides an example of a common credit card disaster scenario. Michael is a senior at Loyola Marymount University in Los Angeles, California. He admitted that he's materialistic. "I want to live the good life," he said. His hunger for the good life helped him in his earlier college days to pack more than a half-dozen pieces of plastic — American Express, Optima, MasterCard, VISA, a department store card, and two gas company cards. His VISA had a $700 credit limit which he maxed out the card the day he got it. In a three month spending spree, his credit card debt mounted to $25,000. Great! Free money, Michael thought. "I didn't know how credit cards worked," he said. "I didn't know anything about interest rates. I didn't even know how to balance a checkbook." With help, Michael began digging himself out of debt — with amazing results.

How? Michael put himself on a cash diet. He cut up his credit cards. Everytime he came across something he liked, he had to ask himself whether he really needed it. Distinguishing between needs and wants is very important. Ninety-nine percent of the time, it is a want, not a need. Whenever a payment is due, make it as soon as possible because most credit card issuers use the average-daily-balance method for computing interest charges. That means each day makes a difference in the interest charged. In Michael's case, he used professional help through Consumer Credit Counseling Service, a non-profit organization that helps people pay their bills and permanently change their attitudes toward money and the way they handle their finances. He also depleted his savings account to pay off his debt and put every cent of money earned in an additional part-time job for two years into paying off his debt.

This is just one example that points out the importance of parents helping their students understand the implications and responsibilities of having credit cards. Learning to manage credit is a part of the basic skills in modern life. You may want to include the following questions in your discussion.

* *Why have a credit card?*
* *How do interest rates work?*
* *When will my credit rating be established?*
* *Can my potential landlord and/or future employer check my credit history?*
* *Explain what a debit card is.*
* *What is Consumer Credit Counseling Service?*

Most of all, teach by example. As Michael now says, "You need only one credit card. That's all my Dad has, and he pays it all off at the end of the month." Michael realized the hard way that there really is no such thing as a free ride.

*"The quality of a person's life does not depend on the circumstances of his life as much as the attitude with which he faces those circumstances."*

- UNKNOWN

# Chapter 7

# CHANGING VALUES AND NECESSARY ADJUSTMENTS

College freshmen are creating their world, and they need space to blossom. Know that you have given them the best you could in helping them structure their own value system. This background will become the core of their decision-making processes. Accept them as they are. As they change, show excitement for them.

College success is not so much a matter of being smart enough as being strong enough. We can interpret this to mean that those students who are less smart but have a clearer sense of their own capacities and capabilities have a better chance of success in college than the very best students who may never have been stretched. Being clear about who they are and their core values is very important. A vision or a personal goal is the single greatest predictor of college success.

All college students face more choices than they ever had before. A few of the choices are mundane: what to eat for lunch, whether to go to classes, when to study, how often to party, and when to go to bed. In addition to these choices, however, come more significant ones that add additional pressures: with whom to be friends, whether to drink alcohol, and whether to have sex. When I speak to high school seniors, I suggest that they decide before they get to college if they are going to be willing to compromise on such issues. How much? A little? A lot? Not at all? Their decisions about these issues are going to influence their choices to a great extent.

Two of the biggest adjustments students will have to make in the first few weeks involve choosing friends and getting along with their roommate. Many students will do anything to feel included as they search for the group of friends with whom they feel most comfortable. For many students, it will be the first time they will have no familiar parental boundaries to keep them in line.

A large percentage of the students I speak to about the college transition have their own room at home; many have their own bathroom; some have their own television, stereo, or car. Many of these students don't know how to share. They may find themselves living in a residence hall with 300 people when they are used to living with five people at home. Having a roommate in college is a tremendous adjustment, and it will be a growth experience. How positive an experience it is depends on the student.

There are generally three different ways of handling problems with roommates. In the first way, one or the other roommate just leaves the room most of the time. In this situation they are avoiding dealing with the problem. The second way is when one roommate goes to the administrator, area coordinator, or counselor to discuss the problem — usually all residence halls have someone to talk to about roommate situations. This occurs more frequently with freshmen during the second month of school. The third way to deal with roommate problems is to both sit down and say, "Look, we've got a problem; I don't like what's going on; let's work it out." It may be little things like borrowing hair dryers, toothpaste, clothes; it may be big things, such as a roommate's girlfriend or boyfriend spending the night in the room.

However they work it out, I tell seniors what one college freshman shared with me about dealing with roommate situations: Do not compromise your values, but compromise. Compromise your situation maybe, but not what you believe in. You have to be strong. Believe in yourself and your values and you will do just fine on the college campus.

Another college freshman commented on making friends as a freshman: For every person that you think doesn't like you because you are not a partyer or you are not in a sorority or fraternity or you are not like them, there are three more people who will like you for just being you.

Living in a residence hall means relating to a new set of peers in a major way. The relationships usually shape themselves in the first few weeks, which for many students, is a time that friendships develop with a roommate or in a suite or somewhere around campus with college activities. The college and university system is set up with many resources that support the students and help them make the transition successfully.

Whether your young adult chooses to room with a best friend, a good friend, match up with someone on the recommendation of mutual friends, or chooses to go "pot luck," meaning being assigned a roommate by the college or university, encourage him or her to make contact with the roommate during the summer. This gives the two young people a chance to write letters, exchange pictures, or talk on the phone. This will help ease some of the anxiety about the roommate.

Students are already wondering who is rooming with people they know and who is going "pot luck?" If you go "pot luck" will he or she be the 4.0 or die type? Will they want to party until dawn? And how in the world will I fit all of my stuff into only half of that tiny room?

Here are some comments about the roommate situation from college freshmen I interviewed. Robert, a freshman at Samford University, roomed with a friend he knew for two years. They were good friends, but not great friends. "We were very different," Robert said. "He was outgoing and used to having a lot of friends around–and he was messy; I was quiet and neat. Sometime he'd walk over people to get what he wanted, but it ended up that we just respected each other. We each sort of changed and got the other one's better qualities. Some of the things he was doing at the beginning he stopped doing as time went on."

Kim, a freshman at UNC, roomed with her best friend. Guidance counselors warned them about doing that because usually one or the other is ready to move on after one semester, but doesn't want to hurt the friend's feelings. The student stays, but is miserable all the while.

I recommend making an agreement to room for one semester or one year, with the stipulation that they will each find other roommates after that time. In this way, feelings aren't hurt and the two can usually remain good friends. They also have more opportunity to go out and make new friends during their college years. In Kim's case, the arrangement worked out the first year. The girls were different, but their values were very similar, which is the reason Kim thinks they succeeded as roommates. They also had some common interests, but some different ones too. They were able to branch out and meet others in the process of pursuing individual niches.

Suzie, a student at the University of Richmond, wondered if anyone would talk to her. She had a choice of rooming with one, two, or three roommates. She chose three roommates. "At least I would get along with one of the three," she said. She ended up liking all her roommates, so her choice was a good one.

Jennifer, a freshman at Guilford College, fought with one of her roommates over the phone bill. Three of the four roommates would pay a share of one bill, and the roommate would send in her check, which eventually bounced. Then the phone was disconnected. Not having a phone is a real problem for a freshman. Jennifer tried working out the problem, but eventually she changed roommates.

Laura, a freshman at Furman University, went "pot luck" and loved her roommate. She arranged to meet her during the summer and this helped lift some of the "roommate anxiety" typical for incoming freshmen.

A freshman at Appalachian State University, Kristin was one of three children. Her roommate was very spoiled because she had no siblings to relate to growing up. Besides, she was used to receiving all the attention in her household. Kristin found it difficult to work things out, but made the best of it. They mutually decided to change roommates the following year, and she and her old roommate became friends. By handling it this way, Kristin had the whole year to meet other people and make the best choice for a roommate.

In most cases, the roommate experience takes time and energy, but it is an important part of the college transition. Students often judge their roommate too soon, and they should realize that it may take a few months to get acquainted. And, as one student from UNC-Greensboro said, "Be tolerant. You are not going to like everything about your roommate, and you might learn something from your differences." You can help by being that listening ear, but do encourage your student to work out the situation.

## Roommate Advice

Students who had completed their freshman year in college shared some additional advice about roommates:

* *Be flexible — "Hope for the best and hold on tight."*
* *Be patient and understanding.*
* *Keep an open mind. "Go into this crazy roommate stuff with an open mind — you'll probably witness a lot of diversity first hand that you may not have experienced in high school."*
* *Be honest from the start.*
* *Set up some rules from the beginning.*

* *Be cooperative, and learn to compromise. "Everything won't be as you expect it, but with time everything will work to your benefit."*
* *Don't judge your roommate too soon. It may take a few months to get acquainted.*
* *Learn to cope no matter what.*
* *Try to meet before school starts.*
* *If you just can't get along, change.*

Parents need to remember that for many college freshmen, sharing a room, bathroom, and telephone is a new experience. Many give up too soon and immediately change roommates. They sometimes miss out on a rich learning experience and the benefits that come from associating with another person who is not exactly like them.

On all campuses I have visited, residence hall counselors are readily available for those who ask for help in working through their roommate problems. Counselors at the student health centers on campus also are available to discuss roommate situations and options in dealing with those situations.

Students usually find that by changing roommates during those first few weeks, their only choices are others who also don't get along with their roommate. If the problems encountered with the roommate are not too great and if they stick it out first semester, they each have time to search for another roommate who may be more compatible.

All of my surveys of college-bound high school seniors indicate that getting along with a roommate is still the number one concern or anxiety among college-bound high school seniors as they look toward their freshman year. Again, as parents, listen, listen, listen, but let your young adult come up with options for a workable solution. Let them work the problems out.

*"You are the bows from which your children as living arrows are sent forth."*
- KAHIL GIBRAN, THE PROPHET

# Chapter 8

# CONNECTING COLLEGE AND CAREER

Did you know that 75 percent of the children now in high school will not obtain a college degree? About 50 percent of high school students will go on to college and about half those will drop out, thus only 25 percent of todays high school students will end up graduating from college. That's one survey.

Another national survey of the 1994 freshmen classes of 4-year institutions shows the nation's lagging retention rate of 73.1 percent. That's a dropout rate of 26.9 percent.

Another interesting statistic: Only 36 percent of incoming freshmen will graduate in five years or less and get a job that requires a degree! The U.S. Labor Department statistics show that the average annual income for a typical college graduate established in the work force is almost double what a high school graduate makes.

And, one last statistic: 25 percent of 25-year olds are now still living with their parents.

Oh what fun!

Now, parents, there are two ways of looking at these statistics in light of the fact that your children are planning to go on to college.

* *The situation is hopeless or*
* *There is a whole lot to do in college to graduate and build toward a successful future.*

So, what can parents do to support their children in meaningful ways? First, in order to make sure they will be marketable when they graduate, we need to know what skills are the most important to learn during their formal college education. And, secondly, what are the best ways for students to acquire these skills during their college years?

## Skills Students Need To Develop In College:

* *Communication skills – written and oral communication.*
* *Ability to work as part of a team — teammanship, learned through extracurricular activities and class projects.*
* *Desire to succeed — this will show up in their grades and will take effective time-management skills — need a schedule from Day 1.*
* *Leadership — seek opportunities no matter how small, learn how to make things happen and move a team forward.*
* *Problem solving — from analytical ability to initiative, imagination and ingenuity; employers always put this skill at the top of the list for potential employees. They want employees who can solve day-to-day problems at work. Employees need to serve customers, and in order to do that, they need the ability to solve their problems.*

Your students can develop all these skills while in college. Whatever they choose, whatever decision they make, encourage them to keep the ultimate goal in their mind: graduation day and connecting to the workforce.

## Majors = Careers ?

Encourage your students to connect to the career center on their campus during their freshman year. Colleges are paying increasing attention to retention and addressing the fact that so many students are not graduating. So, numerous campuses have wonderful centers that encourage freshmen to start career planning during their freshman year. It makes sense.

The relationship of college majors to careers varies. Obviously, if your student wants to become a nurse, he or she needs to major in nursing. Engineers major in engineering. Pharmacists major in pharmacology. They do this in order to be certified as a nurse, engineer, or pharmacist.

Most career fields don't require a specific major. So, nursing, history, engineering, or English majors might choose to become bank managers, sales representatives, career counselors, production managers, or any number of things. And, in most cases, a college major alone is not enough to land a job.

This is where experience and competencies that are related to one's chosen field come in. And, so we move on to what is now called "Experiential Learning," which basically means building a career base through experience.

These learning experiences have many advantages:

* *Incorporates classroom learning with working world experiences.*
* *Helps identify potential career paths and improve career decision making.*
* *Helps pay for college expenses.*
* *Teaches valuable job-search skills.*
* *Provides work experience and improves post-graduation job prospects.*


These hands-on experiences can be found in several ways:

* *Internships during the summer months.*
* *Cooperative Education Programs. The benefits of these programs are that students are paid competitively while gaining practical experience; Co-ops work with the same organizations for 2-3 semesters, which provides for more meaningful relationships with professional staff; and nationally about two thirds of students who Co-op are offered full-time employment with their Co-op employers upon graduation.*
* *Job shadowing. Students learn about various career fields and network with professionals in their disciplines. Observations can be 1-3 days or may be conducting an informational interview about the career field being shadowed.*
* *Volunteering. Employers want to know what else students do on the college campus in addition to their class work. Volunteering is an integral part of the big picture of student life and can enlarge a young person's view of the world of work.*

These are opportunities your students must acquire in order to gain the necessary experience and develop the skills I mentioned earlier. Co-curricular activities also help to develop these skills. Again, these activities broaden the mind and help young people begin to vision the bigger picture. Encourage your student to keep his or her eye on the big picture and keep in mind the ultimate goal with every decision: graduation day and connecting to the workforce.

## Parent Support of Careers

We, as parents, need to be aware of our own biases and perhaps limited knowledge base about careers. In addition to traditional careers, we've seen an explosion of new careers and job titles since the technology revolution. Watch out for myths and misconceptions when your student mentions a new career field. Parents need to listen. If students mention a career field that interests them, they must have heard about it from someone or read about it somewhere. So, encourage them to explore the field and learn more about the career. Show support for their choices. Don't pressure them to change just because it may not be the field you would have chosen for them. In addition, support experiential learning as a way to investigate a potential career. Freshman year is not too early to begin exploring careers — timely involvement is essential. Most of all, be patient with your young adult.

After college graduation, the fears and worries begin again for both parents and students. For parents, these are the major questions:

* *Will my daughter have a job?*
* *Can I handle my son living at home again?*
* *In what ways has the college degree helped my daughter/son with life skills.*

Post-graduation surveys show some students are living at home — with varying degrees of success — after graduating from college. Let me give you two such scenarios. I hear from career counselors on college campuses that when students graduate from college and live at home, some parents charge no rent and the graduates have little, if any, responsibilities. According to these counselors students are in a comfort zone. They live at home and are still working at a local department store as a cashier, for example. It's very comfortable to them and they have no other reason to go out in the workforce to progress and explore possibilities or opportunities. They have some fear of the unknown, but, then the parents also haven't given them that push — it becomes a co-dependency. Sometimes, students may take a year or more to begin exploring what they can do with their major.

A parent can say, "While you're living at home, you are going to pay rent and part of the utilities and part of the food expense." Some ground rules need to be established. The issue is not always the money, but the responsibility and understanding where their paychecks are going. As parents, we need to set the rules to promote life skills and not just to get the rent. With some families, the issue may be that room and board money is needed. If this is the case, still remember to set the rules to promote life skills.

Many parents are asked "How's it going to feel to have your kid graduate?", and many parents respond: "I'll tell you after she or he gets a job." One parent says when her son graduated from college he'd had several job interviews, but nothing had come through for a career job. He was working at the local pizza place in his college town. After discussing the situation with his parents and going into both the pros and cons of various options, he chose to live at home and spend 40 hours a week seeking a career job related to his major and his interests. As a birthday gift, his parents gave him a 14-week Dale Carnegie course, which he was eager to take in order to improve his communication skills. Two months after graduation, he started a full time job that was related to his field of interest. With his confidence bolstered, his excitement was at an all time high.

These examples show how parental communication and advice can be helpful rather than detrimental. Again, be patient. Each student is different and is on a different timetable. Ultimately, however, graduates need to make their own career and life choices.

# Being a College Freshman is Exciting But a Little Bit Scary

New experiences, new friends,
And don't forget THE roommate.

No curfew, no rules, and
What is this thing called time management?

Managing my money.
What money?

Knowledge, 15 hours of classes.
Will I pass?

Stress.
Not a chance.

Independence, freedom.
But I miss my home and family.

Making choices. Parties, alcohol, sex.
What are my values?

Major? Career?
Connect to work?

Because I grew, I learned, I matured.
I laughed, I loved, I prayed.

Being a college freshman is exciting but a little bit scary.

The exciting part won out.
I am now a college sophomore!

-KAYE BERNARD MCGARRY, M.ED.

2001

THE FAMOUS EDUCATOR, JOHN DEWEY, ONCE SAID,

*"Education is not only preparation for life—education is life itself."*

# Chapter 9

# DEALING WITH OUR FEARS

## Parents as Best Friends

My parents were the kind of parents who taught by example. How they lived taught me how to live my life. I don't have many memories of "do this" or "do that." Perhaps it was because I was one of eight children. My parents couldn't get around to everyone all the time. My mother married at 30, which was considered late in her era. She and my Dad were married for 48 years before she died of cancer. I never knew she was suffering; she had Dad's support and suffered in silence. Today, how many of us could raise eight children? In Mom's later years, she was still giving back to her community, by volunteering at the hospital every week. She exercised regularly, prayed, cooked, read books, and worked crossword puzzles. On the day before she died, she played bridge and lunched with friends. Her last words to me were "I love you," and my last words to her were "Mother, I love you, too."

Today, my father is 82 years old; he continues to give support and encouragement in helpful and meaningful ways to his eight children. Recently, when he was visiting us in Charlotte, we were discussing the trials and tribulations of parenting. We talked about my remaining college student—my son Derek, a freshman. My Dad used to say to each of us: Just remember that of all the people in the world, two of the best friends in the world, the only ones you can depend on, are your parents, because they will always do what's best for you. Have belief in these friends. Then, he said to me, "I'm your best friend."

My Dad also said that even during those times when a parent's decision can appear hurtful, through all the tears, the sorrows, the frustrations of teenage life, have faith in your parents. When children finally realize that their parents are their best friends, they will have reached a new level of maturity and happiness. Parenting is not something new. We can learn new techniques from generation to generation, but some things remain the same. Children learn through our example as parents.

In a few weeks, our kids will go off to the college campus as young adults. They have the opportunity for a new beginning. They can write their own chapter in their own book of life. We, as parents, are challenged to let go and bring our communication level with our college students to an adult-to-adult level throughout the college years and beyond. Moms and Dads, ask yourself, "What am I trying to achieve as a parent of a college freshman?"

Will your child eventually be able to say, as I can, and as my three older college graduates, Dennie, Denise, and Deborah Dee are able to say, "My parents *are* my best friends."

## Letting Go

Recently, my husband and I were the parents of a college freshman for the fourth time. We have left two children at the University of North Carolina at Chapel Hill, one at the University of Georgia in Athens, and finally left our youngest at Cornell University, in Ithaca, New York, 700 miles from Charlotte, North Carolina.

I describe my feelings in leaving my fourth child on the campus much like my freshman son described his feelings as we left him—exciting but a little bit scary.

Let's talk about the scary part first. As parents, what are our main concerns? Are we concerned with the safety of our student on campus, as many parents tell me? Do we fear our student will be distracted from our main goal of providing an academic education? Or are we worried that our student now has 24 hours a day, 168 hours a week, to manage, and only about 15 hours in an entire week are scheduled for class time? How is he or she going to manage the other 153 hours in each week without our help?

Probably, though, what scares most of us as parents is a combination of all three issues. Exciting, but a little bit scary?

The other feeling I wrestled with on my way home from Ithaca that September night was the exciting part. Letting go also means changes at home. In my case, the youngest is now the college freshman. I find my daily routine and responsibilities at home have changed quite a bit. My home chores used to revolve around an entire family's needs and now they revolve around just my husband and me.

How nice for those of us who have planned for this moment. My list of goals is endless. I have reevaluated how I spend my time. I am at a crossroad. My volunteer commitments in my community have changed; I have dropped some and added those which are most important to me and are in areas where I can best contribute my talents and skills; I have gradually forged ahead to pursue additional goals that fit into my changing lifestyle.

I am prepared; yet I cannot deny the tears I tried to fight back as I said goodbye to my freshman in Ithaca. And, I'll always remember my parting words to him, "Love ya," and his response, "I love you too."

I didn't want him to see the tears as we stood outside his residence hall in the night, but I can sense he knew what I felt. Letting go is not easy, but it is a necessary step in the life of parents. I need and want to let go to allow him the freedom of writing his own new chapter of his book of life. After all, being a college freshman gives students the opportunity for a new beginning.

I, on the other hand, along with many parents, must also have the freedom to set about writing the next chapter of my book of life. I need to make the most of my opportunity for a new beginning as well. Exciting but a little bit scary? YOU BET!

# Sample Schedule

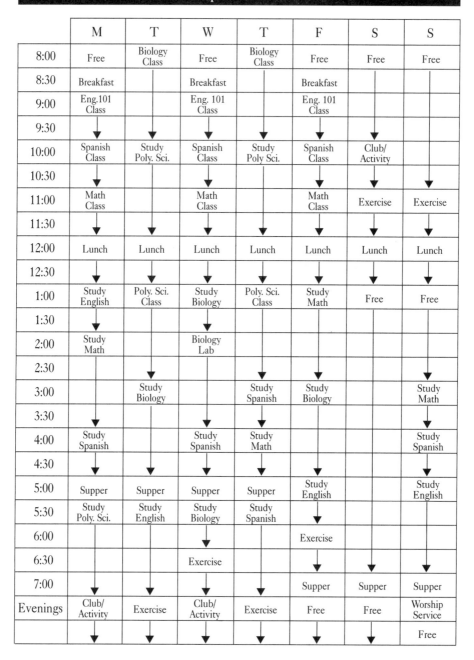

|  | M | T | W | T | F | S | S |
|---|---|---|---|---|---|---|---|
| 8:00 | Free | Biology Class | Free | Biology Class | Free | Free | Free |
| 8:30 | Breakfast | | Breakfast | | Breakfast | | |
| 9:00 | Eng.101 Class | | Eng. 101 Class | | Eng. 101 Class | | |
| 9:30 | | | | | | | |
| 10:00 | Spanish Class | Study Poly. Sci. | Spanish Class | Study Poly Sci. | Spanish Class | Club/ Activity | |
| 10:30 | | | | | | | |
| 11:00 | Math Class | | Math Class | | Math Class | Exercise | Exercise |
| 11:30 | | | | | | | |
| 12:00 | Lunch | Lunch | Lunch | Lunch | Lunch | Lunch | Lunch |
| 12:30 | | | | | | | |
| 1:00 | Study English | Poly. Sci. Class | Study Biology | Poly. Sci. Class | Study Math | Free | Free |
| 1:30 | | | | | | | |
| 2:00 | Study Math | | Biology Lab | | | | |
| 2:30 | | | | | | | |
| 3:00 | | Study Biology | | Study Spanish | Study Biology | | Study Math |
| 3:30 | | | | | | | |
| 4:00 | Study Spanish | | Study Spanish | Study Math | | | Study Spanish |
| 4:30 | | | | | | | |
| 5:00 | Supper | Supper | Supper | Supper | Study English | | Study English |
| 5:30 | Study Poly. Sci. | Study English | Study Biology | Study Spanish | | | |
| 6:00 | | | | | Exercise | | |
| 6:30 | | | Exercise | | | | |
| 7:00 | | | | | Supper | Supper | Supper |
| Evenings | Club/ Activity | Exercise | Club/ Activity | Exercise | Free | Free | Worship Service |
| | | | | | | | Free |

**Effort + Motivation = Academic Success**

## Sample Schedule

|         | M | T | W | T | F | S | S |
|---------|---|---|---|---|---|---|---|
| 8:00    |   |   |   |   |   |   |   |
| 8:30    |   |   |   |   |   |   |   |
| 9:00    |   |   |   |   |   |   |   |
| 9:30    |   |   |   |   |   |   |   |
| 10:00   |   |   |   |   |   |   |   |
| 10:30   |   |   |   |   |   |   |   |
| 11:00   |   |   |   |   |   |   |   |
| 11:30   |   |   |   |   |   |   |   |
| 12:00   |   |   |   |   |   |   |   |
| 12:30   |   |   |   |   |   |   |   |
| 1:00    |   |   |   |   |   |   |   |
| 1:30    |   |   |   |   |   |   |   |
| 2:00    |   |   |   |   |   |   |   |
| 2:30    |   |   |   |   |   |   |   |
| 3:00    |   |   |   |   |   |   |   |
| 3:30    |   |   |   |   |   |   |   |
| 4:00    |   |   |   |   |   |   |   |
| 4:30    |   |   |   |   |   |   |   |
| 5:00    |   |   |   |   |   |   |   |
| 5:30    |   |   |   |   |   |   |   |
| 6:00    |   |   |   |   |   |   |   |
| 6:30    |   |   |   |   |   |   |   |
| 7:00    |   |   |   |   |   |   |   |
| Evenings|   |   |   |   |   |   |   |
|         |   |   |   |   |   |   |   |

Enter:  X for Class time/Lab time
S for Study time (read/outline/review notes)
O for free time
W for Work hours (if applicable)

Effort + Motivation = Academic Success

## Sample Student Budget - Fall Semester

(Approximately 4 months)

|  | Budgeted | Actual |
|---|---|---|
| Books | $200-400 | _____ |
| Lab Fees | 25-50 | _____ |
| Duplicating/Color Copying | 5-30 | _____ |
| Class materials/office supplies/computer disks | 30-60 | _____ |
| Telephone (long distance) | 5-30 | _____ |
| Transportation (Bus pass/gas/taxi) | 20-45 | _____ |
| Dry Cleaning | 5-50 | _____ |
| Laundry (quarters) | 50-200 | _____ |
| Club dues | 20-50 | _____ |
| Snacks (of course) | 150-250 | _____ |
| Lost Room Key | 30 | _____ |
| Stamps | 5-10 | _____ |
| Toiletries (soap/toothpaste/ laundry detergent/cosmetics) | 30-75 | _____ |
| Medical Supplies (tylenol, cold medicine, vitamins) | 15-50 | _____ |
| Gifts & Cards/Family/Friends | 5-100 | _____ |
| Clothes | 50-400 | _____ |
| Entertainment | 200-500 | _____ |
| TOTALS: | 845-2,330 | _____ |

## Gift Ideas For College Freshmen

*. . .birthday, Christmas, Chanukkah, care packages, special occasions. . .*

* Rolls of quarters for laundry/drink machines

* $5.00 gift certificates to food chains - McDonalds, Chilis, Wendys, Burger King, Chick-fil-A

* Gift certificates for gas

* Stamps for postcards and letters

* Streamers/balloons/goodie bag for Halloween or other holidays

* $5.00 phone cards to call friends

* Gift certificates for books or video rentals

* T-shirts or boxers (clothes are something no college student likes to wash, so having extras is a plus)

* Powdered lemonade or fruit drink

* Package of assorted birthday or greeting cards (example: Current Greeting Cards)

* Toiletries such as soap, toothpaste, shampoo, deodorant, laundry detergent

## Responses To Survey Of College Freshmen

**1. Responses to: What was the most effective thing families did to provide encouragement and support as a college freshmen?**

"They did not put pressure on me about grades but supported me all the way. Kept in touch!" —Sally, Furman University

"Let me know I could tell them anything and they would understand. Did not put pressure on me, which made me more responsible and independent." —Sydney, Southern Methodist University

"Everyone in my family called during the first week of school. My parents came to parents' weekend; it showed me they cared about me." —Will, North Carolina State University

"They didn't call me, but told me to call as much as I wanted. Although it was hard on them, it gave me the space I needed, even though I did call almost every day!" —Mebane, University of North Carolina, Chapel Hill

"Let me go. They didn't get sappy and emotional. They were there to listen, but they weren't always all over my back." —Jeff, University of North Carolina, Greensboro

"Encouraged me not to worry about grades as much as growing and learning in a broader sense." —Carlo, Davidson College

"They supported me in all my decisions, even when I dropped a class. They have faith that I am trying hard. They listen to me when I want someone to talk to." — Hunter, Clemson University

"They talked to me through e-mail and sent care packages." —Walter, University of South Carolina

## Responses To Survey Of College Freshmen  cont.

**2. Responses to: What advice can you give to incoming freshmen on how to balance the freedom of college with the structure of home when students return to their families during the first year of college?**

"Be patient with your parents. This is a big change for them as well as for you. No matter what, they are still an important part of your life." —Richard, Duke University

"Realize when you come home that you will probably be expected to follow the same house rules as before you left. Don't fight it!" —Mary, Randolph-Macon University

"Basically, things are going to be the same. Respect your parents no matter what." —Sarah, University of North Carolina, Chapel Hill

"Don't expect to be in your college routine when you come home. Relax and catch up on sleep." —Deborah, University of Georgia

"Just remember that when you're home you have to respect your parents' rules. They will be fair for the most part, and remember, you'll be back at school soon enough where you can do anything anytime." —David, University of North Carolina, Charlotte

"Home is not college. College is not home. It's best to follow any restrictions your parents have and remember that the restrictions are temporary." —Will, North Carolina State University

"Enjoy each and every moment." —Tripp, Wake Forest University

"Sit down and refresh your parents' minds about how college students have a different time schedule. Then find a compromise with the curfew." —Reginald, North Carolina State University

"Don't insist on freedom from your folks. It's new to them. Respect old curfews when you can. Your parents won't change as much or as quickly as you will." — Susan, University of North Carolina, Wilmington

## Action Points for Parents

**P**  Parent the college freshman. They will need support and encouragement in helpful and meaningful ways.

**A**  Attend Parent/Student Orientation to learn about the campus and support services available.

**R**  Relax. Have faith in yourself as parents. You have done your best for 18 years in raising your child. Now it's time to let go and let them try to do their best.

**E**  Expenses. Explain finances to your freshman. Who pays for what? Prepare a sample budget as a basic tool to start planning and discussing finances.

**N**  New beginning for college freshmen—college is a new experience and it is different from high school. Give support, yet create some distance.

**T**  Trust them—
have faith in them and their abilities.

**I**  Initiate new and higher levels of communication patterns with your student before he or she leaves for the college campus, and continue to communicate on an adult-to-adult level throughout the college years.

**N**  Never make judgements; there are no right or wrong answers when it comes to your student learning to set his or her own values, limits, etc.

**G**  Gauge the success of the entire college experience by more than just the first semester.

*"Far away there in the sunshine are my highest aspirations. I may not reach them, but I can look up and see their beauty, believe in them, and try to follow where they lead."*

\- LOUISA MAY ALCOTT

What parents of "soon-to-be" college freshmen said about **A New Beginning: A Survival Guide For Parents Of College Freshmen...**

"Great info — lots of common sense and supportive words."

"I really enjoyed reading this well-written book. It's very thoughtful."

"You have provided me with excellent advice."

**A New Beginning: A Survival Guide For Parents Of College Freshmen** is a very special book for all parents facing major decisions with a child who is about to enter college for the first time. Kaye McGarry, an experienced educational consultant and lecturer on how to survive in college, offers timely and practical suggestions on virtually every aspect of a college student's life. How to manage one's time and finances, how to study, how to set a reasonable budget, and how to relate positively to a new roommate are just a few of the topics covered. More importantly, Ms. McGarry offers guidelines to every parent who must let go in order to establish a new adult to adult relationship with their son or daughter. This book should be "required" reading for any parent whose child is about to enter college for the first time.

> Louis A. Trosch, Sr.
> *Senior Partner of the Law Firm*
> *Conrad, Trosch & Kemmy, P.A.*
> *Full Professor of Business Law*
> *University of North Carolina at Charlotte (UNCC)*

Ms. McGarry has given parents of entering college students a gem. In this small book she draws upon her rich professional and personal experience to cover all the bases for these parents. One might add, for the entering student as well, because for many families it will be of value for all to read it. She gets right to the point in each chapter and provides numerous examples that enrich our understanding of the pertinent issues, such as letting go, when and how to intervene if at all, managing time and studies, budgeting, visiting and the first time home.

During the past decade various books have been published to assist parents and students in coping with the college years. Ms. McGarry's book is a valuable addition, especially because its sole focus is on the first year.

> John E. Reinhold, D.S.W.
> *Senior Clinical Social Worker (retired)*
> *University of North Carolina-Chapel Hill*

# Order Form

**Telephone Orders:**
Call Toll Free:  1-800-280-4880 Ext. 88

**Postal Orders:**
Survival In College Press
5101 Gorham Drive
Charlotte, N.C. 28226-6405

Please send me _____ copies of **A New Beginning: A Survival Guide For Parents Of College Freshmen** at $12.95 per copy. (6 1/2% N.C. Sales Tax included)

Company Name: _____

Name: _____

Address:_____

City: _____State _____Zip _____- _____

**Shipping & Handling**
Book Rate: $3 for the first book and $.75 for each additional book

**Payment**
☐ Check
☐ Money Order

Quantity discounts are available on bulk purchases of this book for educational training purposes, fund raising or gift giving.

## Call *Toll Free* and Order Now!
## 1-800-280-4880 Ext. 88

## or e-mail at kbmcg@carolina.rr.com